MATZAH MEALS

A Passover Cookbook for Kids

by
Judy Tabs and Barbara Steinberg
illustrated by
Chari R. McLean

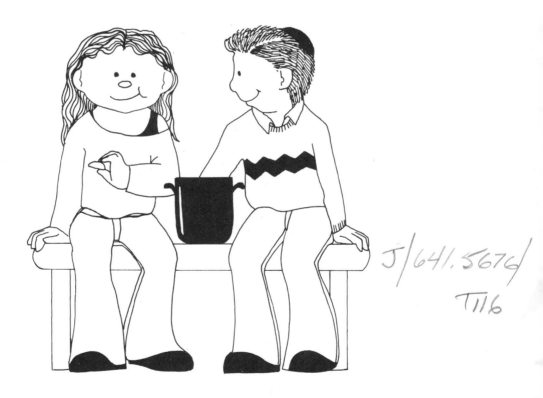

KAR-BEN COPIES, INC.   ROCKVILLE, MD

We dedicate this book to the Tabs Family—Ben, Debbie, and Daniel; to the Steinberg Family—Marvin, Jeffrey, Melanie, Lance, Heidi, Noam, and Jacquie; and to all families at Passover time. May you have the same fond memories of your seders as we have of ours.

A special thanks to our husbands, Ben, for his encouragement, and Marv, for his typing and retyping of the manuscript. This book would not be complete without thanking our moms, Miriam and Anne, for teaching us the meaning of family traditions.

—J.T. and B.S.

Library of Congress Cataloging in Publication Data

Tabs, Judy.
   Matzah meals.

   Summary: A Passover cookbook with an emphasis on matzos and an explanation of the Seder.
   1. Passover cookery—Juvenile literature. 2. Matzos—Juvenile literature. 3. Seder—Juvenile literature.
   [1. Passover cookery. 2. Matzos. 3. Seder]
   I. Steinberg, Barbara. II. McLean, Chari, ill.
   III. Title.
   TX724.T33   1985   641.5′676   85-40
   ISBN 0-930494-44-X

CONTENTS

⌐ some
you've
₁unch,

B

We _____, but please take a minute to read
thes_____ ₃ime in the end, and insure that your
Pass_____ ___ out just right.

- Ask permission to use the kitchen. If you are using sharp knives, the blender, food processor, or stove, make sure that an older person is close by to supervise your cooking.

- Wash your hands, and wear an apron or washable work clothes.

- Read the recipe carefully and check to see that you have all the ingredients.

- Assemble all ingredients and equipment. Recheck the recipe to make sure you have everything.

- Clear a space to work. Keep a sponge handy for unexpected spills.

- Remember these safety tips: Use potholders to handle hot dishes. Turn pot handles toward the back of the stove, so you don't accidentally knock over a hot pot. Pick up knives by the handle, not the blade, and always cut away from yourself. Always wash fresh fruits and vegetables.

- When you're finished, turn off the stove or oven; put away all food; and wash, dry, and put away all equipment. Wipe the counters and sweep the floor. Remember, good cooks always leave the kitchen neat and clean.

USING THIS COOKBOOK

 means very easy. No cooking or baking is required. Even your little brother can help.

 means you may have to chop, slice, use a blender or food processor, or bake.

 means you must use a hot stove to boil or fry. An adult should be present when you make these recipes.

MEAT/DAIRY/PARVE SYMBOLS

 is a meat recipe

 is a dairy recipe

 is a parve recipe (may be eaten with either meat or dairy).

If your family keeps a kosher home, it is important to use the correct dishes and pots in preparing your recipe. Sometimes a dairy dish can be made parve just by using parve margarine instead of butter. These recipes have the symbols D/P. All packaged foods included in the recipes are available labeled "Kosher for Passover."

EQUIPMENT

Cooking goes faster when you have everything ready. Check the equipment list under the ingredients before you start each recipe. These pictures will help you find what you need.

BAKING DISH	PASTRY BRUSH
BEATERS	PLASTIC WRAP
BOWL	PLATE
CAN OPENER	POT
COLANDER	POT HOLDER
COOKIE SHEET	ROASTING PAN
CUTTING BOARD	SCRAPER
FOIL	SPATULA
FOOD PROCESSOR OR BLENDER	SPOON
FORK	SPREADER
FRYING PAN	STRAINER
GRATER	TIMER
KNIFE	TOOTHPICKS
MEASURING CUP AND SPOONS	VEGETABLE PEELER
PAPER TOWEL	WAXED PAPER

THE KIDS' COMPLETE SEDER

Gelfilte Fish Kabobs (p. 19)

Chicken Soup with Matzah Balls (pp. 16-18)

Cranberry Relish (p. 38)

Roast Chicken with Stuffing (p. 47)

Tsimmes (p. 42)

Fruit Compote (p. 36)

Strawberry Layer Cake (p. 60)

Grape Spritzer (p. 71)

THE STORY OF PASSOVER

Passover lasts for a whole week. The holiday begins with a special meal called a seder. We read the story of how the Jewish people were freed from slavery in Egypt. We use a book called a Haggadah.

The Haggadah tells us that many years ago in the land of Egypt, there lived a mean king called Pharaoh. The Jewish people who lived in Egypt were slaves. They had to work very hard building cities and palaces for Pharaoh. Pharaoh was especially mean to Jewish children. One mother put her baby boy in a basket in the river so Pharaoh wouldn't find him. When Pharaoh's daughter saw the baby, she took him out of the river and saved him. She named him Moses.

When Moses grew up, he saw how cruelly the Jewish slaves were treated and decided to leave Egypt. He became a shepherd in a faraway land. One day, while he was watching his sheep, he heard the voice of God telling him to go back to Egypt and free the Jewish people. Moses went to Pharaoh and asked him to let the Jewish people go. Pharaoh refused. God was angry and punished Pharaoh ten times. Finally, Pharaoh told Moses to take his people out of Egypt.

The Jews left in a hurry and didn't have time to bake their bread in an oven. They put the dough on their backs, and while they were walking, the sun baked it into hard crackers (matzah). Moses led the Jewish people out of Egypt, across the sea, and into the desert. The Jews were happy to be saved. Moses told them to celebrate Passover every year to remember that once they were slaves, but God helped them become free.

SEDER SYMBOLS

Special foods on the Seder table remind us of the Passover story:

MATZAH   Reminds us that the Jews had to leave Egypt quickly and had no time to bake bread. One matzah is the Afikomen, which we hide as a seder game.

GREENS   Parsley or celery—remind us that Passover comes in the spring when everything begins to grow.

SALT WATER   Reminds us of the tears of the Jewish slaves in Egypt.

CHAROSET   A mixture of apples, nuts, and wine—reminds us of the mortar the Jews used to make bricks to build Pharaoh's cities.

MAROR   A bitter vegetable like horseradish—reminds us of the bitter way Pharaoh treated the Jewish people.

ROASTED EGG   Reminds us of the new life that grows in spring.

BONE   Reminds us of the roasted lamb the Jewish people ate when they celebrated the first Passover.

CUP OF ELIJAH   There is a legend that the prophet Elijah visits each seder to wish us a year of peace.

WINE   A symbol of holiday joy.

SETTING THE SEDER TABLE

The seder is a wonderful celebration, and it is fun to make our dinner table beautiful. Help choose a pretty tablecloth or placemats. Buy fresh flowers, or make colorful paper ones for a centerpiece. This is what you'll need for the Seder:

At each place:

- Plate, silverware, napkin
- Wine glass
- Haggadah

On the table:

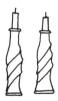

- Candles to welcome the holiday
- Wine or grape juice—enough for four cups for each person
- Three matzah—covered with a matzah cover or napkin
- Cups of salt water for dipping the parsley

For the leader of the seder:

- A pillow for reclining

For the seder plate:

- Greens
- Charoset
- Bitter herb
- Roasted Egg
- Roasted Bone

(Recipes for these foods are on pages 11-13.)

ROASTED EGG AND BONE

What You Need:

1 egg
1 shankbone (or other bone)

Pin
Roasting pan
Potholder
Timer

What You Do:

1. Prick the egg with a pin to let steam escape while cooking.

2. Put egg and bone on baking sheet and roast at 300° for one hour.

HORSERADISH

What You Need:

½ lb. horseradish root
1-2 beets (optional)
1 tsp. vinegar
1 tsp. sugar

Vegetable peeler
Knife
Blender or food processor
Measuring spoon

What You Do:

1. Scrape horseradish root and cut into chunks. If you want red horseradish, scrape beets and cut into chunks, also.

2. Put chunks into blender or food processor. Add vinegar and sugar.

3. Blend a few seconds until chopped. Don't overblend.

CHAROSET

What You Need:

3 apples
1 tsp. cinnamon
½ cup chopped nuts
2 Tbsp. sweet red wine

Bowl
Vegetable peeler
Measuring spoon
Knife
Chopper

What You Do:

1. Peel apples, remove cores, and slice into a bowl.
2. Add nuts and cinnamon and chop until fine.
3. Add wine and mix.

   Serves 6-8

GREENS (KARPAS)

What You Need:

Parsley, celery, or lettuce

Knife

What You Do:

Cut into bite-size pieces and place on the Seder Plate.

SALT WATER

What You Need:

1 cup cold water
1 tsp. salt

Measuring cup
Measuring spoon

What You Do:

Put cold water in small pitcher or cup. Add salt. You may wish to make several cups to place around the table.

MATZAH*

What You Need:

2 cups unbleached flour
½ cup water (more if needed)

Mixing bowl and spoon
Rolling pin
Baking sheet
Fork
Spatula
Potholder
Timer

*The requirements for making matzah are very stringent, and some rabbis do not consider home-baked matzah "kosher" for Passover.

What You Do:

1. Preheat oven to 450°.
2. Place flour in bowl.
3. Make a well (hole) in the middle of the flour and pour in water. Mix.
4. Add more water as needed until all the flour is mixed. Use your hands... it's fun! Knead dough until soft, not sticky.
5. Roll into a ball. Divide into quarters.
6. Roll each quarter into a circle. Place matzah on baking sheet and prick all over with a fork. Bake for 5 minutes on each side, or until edges are golden.

Makes 4 matzah

13

SEDER TABLE CRAFTS

SEDER PLATE

Decorate a paper plate with Pesach symbols. Glue foil muffin cups to the plate, and fill with individual portions of parsley, charoset, egg, maror, and bone. Give one to every guest.

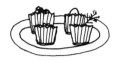

KIDDUSH CUP OR CUP FOR ELIJAH

Cover two paper cups (a size apart) with foil. Glue them bottom to bottom. The smaller one is the stem of your wine cup.

PLACE CARDS

Fold index cards in half. Decorate with pictures of Pesach symbols or spring flowers, and write each guest's name on a card.

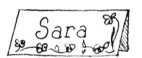

MATZAH COVER

Sew four pieces of felt or cloth together leaving one side open to insert the three matzot. To decorate the top cloth, color with crayon, cover with waxed paper, and iron to set the design. Make a matching afikomen bag.

PILLOW COVER

Draw, paint, or embroider Pesach symbols on a special pillow case to cover the Seder pillow.

SOUPS AND APPETIZERS

CHICKEN SOUP FOR BEGINNERS

What You Need:

2 chicken boullion cubes
1 quart (4 cups) water
2 carrots
2 stalks of celery
½ tsp. dry dill

Pot with cover
Measuring cup and spoon
Vegetable peeler
Knife and cutting board
Potholder
Timer

What You Do:

1. Put the boullion cubes in the water and bring to a boil.
2. Wash and cut up carrots and celery. Add to boiling soup.
3. Add dill.
4. Cover and cook over low heat (simmer) until vegetables are soft, about 20 minutes.

Serves 4

CHICKEN SOUP FOR EXPERTS

What You Need:

1 cut up chicken
2 quarts water
3 celery stalks, including leaves
1 onion
3-4 peeled carrots
1 Tbsp. salt
2-3 shakes of pepper
1 bay leaf (optional)

Large pot with cover
Measuring cup and spoons
Vegetable peeler
Knife and cutting board
Strainer and storage container
Potholder
Timer

What You Do:

1. Cover chicken with water and bring to a boil.
2. Add vegetables and spices.
3. Cover and cook over low heat (simmer) for 1½ hours, until chicken is soft.
4. Cool and strain. Return vegetables and chicken to soup.
5. Soup is best if refrigerated overnight. Skim off fat before reheating and serving.

Serves 8

EASY MATZAH BALLS

What You Need:

2 Tbsp. oil
2 eggs, slightly beaten
½ cup matzah meal
1 tsp. salt
1 Tbsp. water or chicken soup

Bowl
Measuring cup and spoons
Fork, spoon
Plastic wrap
Pot with cover
Potholder/Timer

What You Do:

1. Mix oil and eggs together in a bowl.
2. Add matzah meal and salt. Mix well. Add water and mix again.
3. Cover with plastic wrap and refrigerate for ½ hour.
4. Fill a large pot half full with water and bring to a boil.
5. Wet your hands and take about a tablespoon of mixture and roll into a ball. Drop into boiling water. Reduce heat to a slow boil. Cook covered for 30-40 minutes.
6. Remove from water and serve with chicken soup.

   Makes 10-12

GEFILTE FISH KABOBS

What You Need:

1 jar gefilte fish tidbits
1 small can pineapple chunks
Cherry tomatoes
Lettuce
Horseradish (optional)

_____

Toothpicks
Can opener
Fork or spoon
Serving platter

What You Do:

1. Place a fish tidbit, a pineapple chunk, and a cherry tomato on a toopthpick.

2. Arrange kabobs on a bed of lettuce. Serve with horseradish.

VEGGIES AND DIP

Dippers:

Cherry tomatoes
Broccoli and cauliflower cut into florettes
Carrot and celery cut into sticks
Cucumber slices

Bowl
Knife, fork, spoon
Peeler
Measuring cup and spoon

Pineapple Dip

Mix ¼ cup crushed pineapple with 2 teaspoons of mayonnaise.

Onion Dip

Mix 1 cup sour cream with a package of Passover onion soup mix.

Cucumber Dip

Mash 8 oz. package cream cheese* with dash of grated onion and one grated and strained cucumber.

Cheesy-Nut Dip

Mash 3 oz. package cream cheese* with ¼ cup chopped walnuts.

*Let cream cheese soften at room temperature for about an hour before using.

BREAKFAST
BRUNCH
AND
LUNCH

GRANOLA

What You Need:

4 cups matzah farfel
½ cup nuts
¾ cup shredded coconut
½ cup honey
½ cup oil
½ cup raisins

_____

Measuring cup
Mixing bowl and spoon
Baking sheet/Potholder
Storage container with cover

What You Do:

1. Preheat oven to 350°.

2. Mix farfel, nuts, and coconut in a bowl. Add honey and oil and mix well.

3. Spread mixture on baking sheet. Bake 30 minutes. Stir frequently. Cool.

4. Add raisins and mix. Store in covered container.

   8-10 servings

MATZAH MEAL LATKES

What You Need:

½ cup matzah meal
½ tsp. salt
1 tsp. sugar
¾ cup cold water
3 eggs
Oil for frying

Measuring cups and spoons
Mixing bowl
Frying pan (or griddle) and
   spatula
Mixer (for extra light latkes)
Potholder

What You Do:

1. Mix matzah meal, salt, and sugar together in a bowl.
2. Add eggs and water, and mix well.
3. Heat oil in frying pan. Drop by tablespoons into pan, and brown on both sides.

For extra-light latkes:

1. After step 1 above, separate the eggs (let an adult help you). Beat yolks and add water. Add matzah meal mixture to yolks. Let stand for 1 hour.
2. Beat egg whites until stiff, and add to batter. Fry as directed above.

Serves 3-4

SCRAMBLED EGGS

What You Need:

2 eggs
1 Tbsp. cold water or milk
1 Tbsp. butter or margarine
Salt and pepper to taste

_____

Small bowl and fork
Frying pan
Measuring spoon
Potholder

What You Do:

1. Beat eggs and water (or milk) until fluffy. Add salt and pepper.
2. Put butter or margarine in frying pan and melt over medium heat.
3. Pour eggs into pan and stir until set.

Serves 1

COTTAGE CHEESE PANCAKES

What You Need:

1 cup cottage cheese
2 eggs, beaten
¼ cup matzah meal
1 Tbsp. sugar
¼ tsp. salt
Butter or margarine for frying

_____

Bowl and spoon
Measuring cup and spoons
Frying pan and spatula
Potholder

What You Do:

1. Mix all ingredients in a bowl.
2. Melt butter or margarine in frying pan over medium heat.
3. Drop by tablespoons onto hot frying pan. Brown on both sides.
4. Serve with jelly or sour cream.

Serves 2-3

MATZAH BREI

What You Need:

4 matzah
3 eggs, beaten
½ cup milk
3 Tbsp. oil or margarine

Measuring cup and spoons
Mixing bowl and spoon
Frying pan and spatula
Potholder

What You Do:

1. Crumble matzah into bowl. Add eggs and milk and mix well. Let stand for five minutes to soften matzah.

2. Heat oil in a frying pan. Put matzah mixture into pan and fry on both sides until crisp. Top with jelly or cinnamon-sugar mix.

Serves 4

FRENCH TOAST

What You Need:

1 egg
1 Tbsp. milk
Pinch of salt
1 matzah
1 Tbsp. butter or margarine

_____

Mixing bowl and spoon
Measuring spoon
Frying pan and spatula
Potholder

What You Do:

1. Beat egg with milk and salt.

2. Break matzah into quarters and dip each piece into the mixture.

3. Melt butter or margarine in frying pan. Fry matzah on both sides until brown. Serve hot with sugar, syrup, honey, or butter.

Serves 1-2

PASSOVER SANDWICH ROLLS

What You Need:

½ cup water
⅓ cup oil
1 cup matzah meal
2 tsp. sugar
¼ tsp. salt
2 eggs
Margarine for greasing cookie
   sheet

Measuring cup and spoons
Mixing bowl and spoon
Pot
Baking sheet
Timer/Potholder

What You Do:

1. Preheat oven to 375°.
2. Put water and oil in a pot and bring to a boil. Cool.
3. Mix matzah meal, salt and sugar in a bowl. Pour water and oil over it. Mix well.
4. Add eggs, one at a time, and mix well. Let stand for 15 minutes.
5. Grease hands with oil and form mixture into 6-8 balls. Place on greased cookie sheet and flatten.
6. Bake for 40 minutes until golden brown.

Makes 6-8 rolls

SPREADS

CREAM CHEESE AND JELLY:

Spread cream cheese on matzah or roll. Top with your favorite jam or jelly.

HONEY BUTTER:

Mix ¼ cup of softened butter or margarine with 4 tablespoons of honey. Spread on matzah, rolls, or Passover pancakes.

CINNAMON/SUGAR:

Spread matzah or roll with butter or margarine. Mix ¼ cup sugar with ¼ teaspoon cinnamon and sprinkle some on top.

ONION:

Cut onion in half and rub the cut edge over matzah. Sprinkle with salt and pepper and toast in warm oven. Spread with butter or margarine and serve warm.

Bowl and spoon
Measuring cup and spoon

FILLINGS

TUNA SALAD

What You Need:

1 can tuna fish
2 Tbsp. mayonnaise
1 stalk celery, diced (optional)

Serves 2-3

What You Do:

Put tuna in a bowl. Mix with mayonnaise (and celery). Spread on matzah or roll.

EGG SALAD

What You Need:

2 eggs
2 Tbsp. mayonnaise
Salt and pepper

Serves 2

What You Do:

1. Put eggs in pot and cover with cold water. Bring to a boil. Turn off heat and let eggs sit 20 minutes. Run under cold water to cool.

2. Peel eggs. Cut into quarters, and put in a bowl. Mash with mayonnaise, salt, and pepper. Spread on matzah or rolls.

Can opener
Bowl
Fork, knife, spoon
Measuring spoon

GRILLED CHEESE SANDWICH

What You Need:

Matzah
Sliced cheese
Butter or margarine

_____

Baking sheet
Knife

What You Do:

1. Preheat oven to 400°.
2. Butter matzah and top with sliced cheese. Put on baking sheet and place in hot oven for a minute or two until cheese melts.

Serves 1

"UNSANDWICHES"

APPLE

Cut apple into wedges. Remove core. Spread with cream cheese. Top with jelly.

WALNUT

Add ¼ teaspoon brown sugar and ½ cup raisins to 3 oz. softened creamed cheese. Spread some on half a walnut. Cover with the other half.

BANANA

Peel a banana and slice in half the long way. Spread jam on one half. Top with other half. Cut into bite-size pieces.

FRUITS AND VEGGIES

BABY MOSES SALAD

What You Need:

Basket . . . . Lettuce leaf
Body . . . . Fresh or canned peach half
Arms and legs . . . . Small celery sticks
Head . . . . Large marshmallow
Mouth . . . . Sliced cherry
Hair . . . . Shredded cheese
Eyes, nose . . . . Raisins

_____

Plate
Knife

What You Do:

Place peach half and marshmallow on large lettuce leaf. Decorate with other ingredients.

Serves 1

WALDORF SALAD

What You Need:

1 can tuna, drained
1¼ c. diced apple
2 Tbsp. lemon juice
¼ c. finely chopped celery
2 Tbsp. chopped nuts
3 Tbsp. salad dressing

Can opener
Measuring cup and spoons
Mixing bowl and spoon
Knife and cutting board

What You Do:

1. Mix tuna and apple in a bowl.
2. Sprinkle with lemon juice.
3. Add remaining ingredients and mix well.

Serves 2-4

FRUIT COMPOTE

What You Need:

3 cups of sliced fresh or canned fruit (pineapple,
peaches, pears, apples,
oranges, grapes, apricots,
etc.)
1 Tbsp. lemon juice
3 Tbsp. honey

Glass bowl
Strainer or colander
Spoon
Knife and cutting board
Measuring cup and spoon
Plastic wrap

What You Do:

1. Open and drain canned fruit. Put in
   bowl.
2. Slice fresh fruit and add it to bowl.
3. Stir in lemon juice and honey.
4. Cover with plastic wrap and
   refrigerate before serving.

   Serves 4-6

FRUIT KABOBS

What You Need:

Any or all of the following
  fruits:
Apple slices
Raisins
Orange sections
Grapes
Pineapple cubes
Melon Balls
Prunes

_____

Toothpicks
Serving plate

What You Do:

Select two or three pieces of fruit and
place them on a toothpick. Arrange
kabobs on serving plate.

CRANBERRY RELISH

What You Need:

2 cans whole cranberry sauce
2 cans crushed pineapple
1 package frozen strawberries,
   thawed
1 can mandarin oranges

Strainer or colander
Can opener
Bowl
Plastic wrap
Spoon

What You Do:

1. Put a strainer or colander in your sink.

2. Pour all ingredients into colander and drain.

3. Transfer fruit to a bowl, cover with plastic wrap, and refrigerate before serving.

   Serves 10-12

APPLESAUCE

What You Need:

8 tart apples
1-2 tsp. cinnamon
2-3 cups water
¾ cup sugar

Peeler and knife
Measuring cup and spoon
Baking dish and cover or foil
Strainer
Spoon
Potholder/Timer

What You Do:

1. Preheat oven to 350°.
2. Wash and cut apples into quarters. Place in baking dish. Add cinnamon and water.
3. Cover and bake until soft, about 20 minutes.
4. Put through strainer, add sugar, and mix.
5. Serve warm or cold.

Serves 6-8

CARROT-RAISIN SALAD

What You Need:

1 bag (1 lb.) carrots
1 cup raisins
½ cup mayonnaise

_____

Vegetable peeler
Measuring cup
Blender or food processor
Mixing bowl and spoon

What You Do:

1. Wash and scrape carrots. Cut into slices.
2. Shred carrot slices, using food processor, blender, or grater.
3. Combine shredded carrots, raisins, and mayonnaise in bowl. Chill.

   Serves 6-8

BLENDER POTATO PANCAKES

What You Need:

2 eggs
1 small onion, quartered
1½ tsp. salt
3-4 medium potatoes, cut into
   small pieces
¼ cup matzah meal
¼ cup oil for frying

___

Blender or food processor
Mixing spoon and bowl
Frying pan and spatula
Paper towels/Potholder
Knife and cutting board
Measuring cup and spoon

What You Do:

1. Put all ingredients except oil into blender or food processor for five seconds, or until lumps disappear.
2. Heat oil in frying pan.
3. Drop by spoonfuls into pan, and fry over medium heat until brown on both sides
4. Drain on paper towel.
5. Serve with applesauce.

   Serves 3-4

EASY TSIMMES

What You Need:

1 large can of sliced carrots
1 large can of sweet potatoes
3 apples
½ cup sugar
3 Tbsp. soft margarine
1 cup water
Salt and pepper

Peeler
Knife and cutting board
Can opener
Strainer or colander
Measuring cup and spoon
Baking pan
Foil Wrap
Timer
Potholder

What You Do:

1. Preheat oven to 350°.
2. Open cans and drain carrots and potatoes.
3. Peel, core and slice apples.
4. Arrange vegetables and apples in shallow baking pan.
5. In a bowl, mix together sugar, margarine, water, salt and pepper, and pour over vegetables and apples.
6. Cover pan with foil and bake at 350° for 30 minutes.

   Serves 4-6

MEAT MEALS

HOT DOG KABOBS

What You Need:

1 hot dog
4 cherry tomatoes
½ green pepper, cut into 4
   chunks

Toothpicks
Baking sheet
Knife and cutting board
Potholder/Timer

What You Do:

1. Cut hot dog into 4 pieces. Put one slice on each toothpick. Add cherry tomato and green pepper chunk to each.

2. Broil in oven or toaster oven for 5 minutes or until hot dog browns.

   Serves 1

MEATBALLS

What You Need:

1 lb. ground beef
1 small onion, diced
1 egg
2 Tbsp. water
1 15-oz. can tomato sauce

Mixing bowl and spoon
Knife and cutting board
Measuring spoons
Saucepan with lid
Can opener
Potholder

What You Do:

1. Put meat, onion, egg, and water in a bowl and mix well.

2. Put tomato sauce in saucepan and heat. Wet hands and form meatballs. Drop into sauce. Cover and simmer for 45 minutes.

Serves 3-4

CHICKEN SHAKE

What You Need:*

1 chicken, cut into serving
  pieces
½ cup Italian salad dressing
1 cup matzah meal
Salt, pepper, paprika, garlic
  powder

Mixing bowl and spoon
Measuring cup
Plastic bag
Roasting pan
Potholder/Timer

What You Do:

1. Preheat oven to 375°.
2. Put chicken pieces in shallow bowl. Pour salad dressing over chicken and stir until all the pieces are covered.
3. Put matzah meal and spices into plastic bag. Add chicken pieces, two at a time. Hold bag closed and shake to coat chicken. Arrange coated pieces in one layer in roasting pan.
4. Bake for 45 minutes to 1 hour.

Shortcut: Buy prepared Passover chicken coating and follow package directions.

Serves 4

46

ROAST CHICKEN WITH STUFFING

What You Need:

Whole chicken
Farfel Stuffing Mix
Package mixed dried diced fruit
1 cup raisins

Bowl and spoon
Measuring cup and spoon
Roasting pan
Potholder
Timer

What You Do:

1. Prepare stuffing from directions on the package. Mix in fruit and raisins.
2. Stuff chicken. Bake for 1½ hours at 350°.
3. You may bake stuffing separately in a baking pan for 45 minutes at 350°.

SALAMI LATKES

What You Need:

2 eggs
½ cup matzah meal
½ cup water
½ cup diced salami or bologna
Oil for frying

Measuring cup
Mixing bowl and spoon
Frying pan and spatula
Potholder

What You Do:

1. Beat eggs. Add water and matzah meal and mix well. Add salami and mix again.

2. Heat oil in frying pan. Drop batter by spoonfuls into pan. Fry until brown on both sides.

3. Drain on paper towel. Serve with applesauce.

Serves 2

INTERNATIONAL MATZAH MEALS

MATZAH PIZZA

What You Need:

1 round tea matzah (or regular matzah)
3-4 Tbsp. tomato sauce
2-3 slices cheese
Oregano, garlic powder, to taste (optional)
Oil for baking sheet

_____

Baking sheet
Spoon and knife
Spatula
Potholder/Timer

What You Do:

1. Preheat oven to 350°.
2. Spread tomato sauce on matzah. Top with sliced cheese. Sprinkle with spices.
3. Put matzah on oiled baking sheet. Bake for about 5 minutes or until cheese melts.

   Serves 1

TOSTADO

What You Need:

1 round tea matzah (or regular matzah)
2 slices cheese, cut up
1 Tbsp. oil
¼ cup shredded lettuce
¼ cup cubed tomato
1 Tbsp. scallions
1 Tbsp. green pepper
1 Tbsp. sour cream

Knife and cutting board
Baking sheet
Spoon
Potholder/Timer
Spatula

What You Do:

1. Preheat oven to 300°.
2. Brush matzah with oil and warm in oven for 5 minutes.
3. Cover with cheese and vegetables. Top with sour cream.

   Serves 1

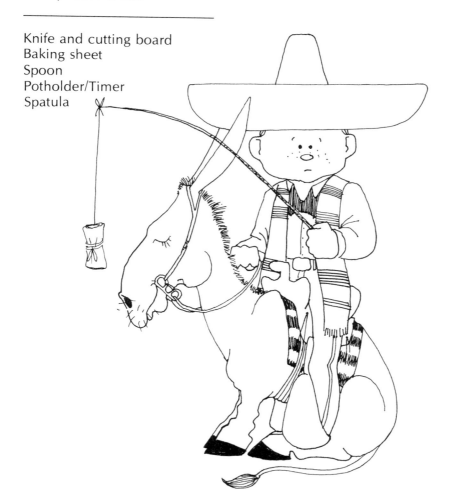

FINGER-DIPPING FONDUE

What You Need:

2 matzah
4 oz. processed cheese
½ cup milk
Salt, pepper, paprika

_____

Saucepan or double boiler
Wooden spoon
Plates and bowls

What You Do:

1. Break matzah into bite-size pieces and arrange on four small plates.

2. Melt cheese over low heat (or on top of double boiler). Add milk and seasoning. Stir with wooden spoon until smooth.

3. Pour cheese mixture into 4 small bowls and put each bowl on a plate of matzah. This is finger-dipping fun!

Serves 4

MATZAH EGG FOO YOUNG

What You Need:

¼ cup mushrooms, sliced
1 onion, chopped
½ cup chopped celery
2 carrots, grated
1 package frozen chopped
  spinach
3 eggs
¾ cup matzah meal
1 tsp. salt
1 dash pepper
2 Tbsp. butter or margarine
Oil for frying

Covered saucepan
Colander
Grater
Knife, spoon
Frying pan and spatula
Measuring cup and spoons
Peeler

What You Do:

1. Cook and drain spinach according to package directions.

2. In a frying pan, saute mushrooms, onion, celery, and carrots in margarine until soft (5-8 minutes). Cool.

3. Add spinach, eggs, matzah meal, salt and pepper and mix well. Refrigerate 15 minutes.

4. Form into pancakes and fry in hot oil until brown on both sides.

   Serves 3-4

HAWAIIAN MATZAH FRY

What You Need:

5 matzah
1 cup crushed pineapple
¼ cup shredded coconut
3 eggs
2-3 Tbsp. margarine
2 Tbsp. sugar
¼ tsp. cinnamon

_____

2 bowls
Spoon
Frying pan, spatula
Measuring cup and spoons

What You Do:

1. Crumble matzah into bowl and add pineapple with juice.
2. Beat eggs and add to matzah. Stir in coconut.
3. Heat butter or margarine in frying pan. Pour in matzah mixture and brown on both sides. Sprinkle with cinnamon sugar.

Serves 4-6

DESSERTS AND SNACKS

CHOCOLATE CHIP COOKIES

What You Need:

2 eggs
½ cup sugar
½ cup margarine, melted
1 cup matzah meal
2 tsp. potato starch
1 6-oz. package chocolate
  chips (or chopped chocolate
  bar)

_____

Bowl/Mixing spoon
Egg beater
Measuring cup and spoon
Cookie sheet
Spatula
Potholder/Timer

What You Do:

1. Preheat oven to 350°.
2. Beat eggs and sugar together in large bowl.
3. Add melted margarine and mix.
4. Add matzah meal, potato starch, and chocolate chips. Mix well.
5. Drop by teaspoonfuls onto ungreased cookie sheet.
6. Bake for 30 minutes.

   Makes 2 dozen

PESACH ICE-BOX COOKIES

What You Need:

¼ lb. margarine
1 cup sugar
1 egg
1 Tbsp. orange juice
¼ tsp. salt
1 cup cake meal
½ cup chopped nuts

Mixing bowl and spoon
Measuring cup and spoon
Knife
Waxed paper
Cookie sheet
Spatula
Potholder/Timer

What You Do:

1. Put sugar and margarine in a bowl. Cream until smooth.

2. Add eggs and juice and beat well. Fold in dry ingredients and nuts.

3. Shape dough into sausages, wrap in waxed paper, and refrigerate for 2 or more hours. (The dough will keep for several days.)

4. Preheat oven to 350°. Slice dough into rounds and bake on ungreased cookie sheet for 15 minutes or until golden.

   Makes 3 dozen

MERINGUE KISSES

What You Need:

½ cup sugar
3 eggs
Chocolate chips
Margarine (to grease
  cookie sheet)

___

Egg beater
Mixing bowl and spoon
Measuring cup
Cookie sheet
Spatula
Potholder/Timer

What You Do:

1. Preheat oven to 350°.
2. Separate eggs (ask a grownup to help you) and save yolks for another use.
3. Beat egg whites until foamy.
4. Gradually beat in sugar and continue beating until egg whites are stiff and stand in peaks.
5. Drop by teaspoonfuls onto greased cookie sheet.
6. Put a chocolate chip on top of each.
7. Bake 30 minutes or until meringue kisses are hard.

   Makes 12-18

QUICK MACAROONS

What You Need:

5 cups flaked coconut
1 can (14 oz.) sweetened
   condensed milk
1 tsp. vanilla
½ cup chopped nuts
Margarine (to grease cookie
   sheet)

Bowl
Measuring cup and spoon
Cookie sheet
Spatula
Potholder/Timer
Can opener

What You Do:

1. Preheat oven to 350°.
2. Mix ingredients together in bowl. Make sure they are mixed well.
3. Drop by teaspoonfuls onto lightly greased cookie sheet.
4. Bake for about 15 minutes or until lightly browned.

   Makes 3 dozen

QUICK STRAWBERRY LAYER CAKE

What You Need:

1 sponge cake
1 jar strawberry jelly
1 package fresh or frozen
   strawberries

_____

Serving dish
Knife

What You Do:

1. Cut sponge cake in half lengthwise.
2. Place one layer on a serving dish. Spread strawberry jelly and top with strawberries.
3. Place second layer on top and repeat.

   Serves 6-8

APPLE CAKE

What You Need:

3 eggs
¾ cup sugar
½ cup oil
⅔ cup cake meal
½ cup potato starch
3 apples, peeled and sliced
   thin
3 Tbsp. sugar
½ tsp. cinnamon
Margarine (to grease pan)

———————————————

Bowl/Spoon
Egg beater
Measuring cup and spoons
Knife and cutting board
Peeler
8″ cake pan
Potholder/Timer

What You Do:

1. Preheat oven to 325°.
2. In a large bowl, beat eggs until foamy.
3. Add ¾ sugar, oil, cake meal, and potato starch. Mix well.
4. Place apple slices in greased baking dish. Mix 3 Tbsp. sugar and cinnamon and sprinkle over apples.
5. Pour batter over apples.
6. Bake for one hour.
   Serves 10-12

FROZEN FRUIT YOGURT POPSICLES

What You Need:

2 cups plain yogurt
1 small can frozen concen-
   trated fruit juice (orange
   or pineapple)
2 tsp. vanilla

_____

Bowl and spoon
Popsicle holders or
Paper cups
Popsicle sticks
Measuring cup and spoon

What You Do:

1. Thaw frozen juice.
2. Combine all ingredients in a bowl and mix well.
3. Pour into popsicle holders or paper cups. (If you use cups, wait until pops are almost frozen, then put in sticks). You can also make "cube" pops in ice cube trays.

STRAWBERRY ICE CREAM

What You Need:

2 eggs
¼ cup sugar
1 package frozen strawberries
Pinch of salt

_____

Bowl and spoon
Egg beater
Freezer container
Measuring cup

What You Do:

1. Separate eggs (ask a grownup to help) and save yolks for another use.

2. Beat egg whites until stiff. Beat in sugar.

3. Add berries and salt and mix well.

4. Pour into freezer container and freeze. Thaw slightly before serving.

Serves 2-3

CHOCOLATE MATZAH

What You Need:

1 large package chocolate
   chips (or 12 oz. chopped
   chocolate bar)
1 Tbsp. margarine
4 matzah

_____

Saucepan or double boiler
Cookie sheet
Waxed paper
Mixing spoon, rolling pin
Measuring spoon

What You Do:

1. Melt chocolate and margarine over
   low heat. Stir to prevent burning.
2. Break matzah into pieces and stir into
   chocolate.
3. Cover a cookie sheet with waxed
   paper.
4. Pour chocolate matzah mixture onto
   waxed paper and cover with another
   sheet of waxed paper.
5. Flatten mixture with rolling pin.
   Refrigerate.
6. When mixture hardens, peel off top
   paper and break chocolate into
   pieces.

T.V. MUNCH

What You Need:

1 cup dried apples
1 cup dried pears
1 cup dried pineapple
1 cup raisins
1 cup almonds or walnuts, shelled
1 cup chocolate bits

_____

Bowl

What You Do:

1. Put all ingredients in a bowl and mix.
2. Turn on T.V. and munch!

CHOCOLATE NUT BARK

What You Need:

12 ounces semi-sweet
   chocolate bits (or chopped
   chocolate bar)
1 cup whole almonds

Saucepan or double boiler
Cookie sheet
Waxed paper
Mixing spoon
Measuring cup

What You Do:

1. Melt chocolate bits over low heat. Stir to prevent burning.
2. Toast almonds until light brown (you can use toaster oven), and add to chocolate.
3. Spread mixture over cookie sheet lined with waxed paper.
4. Chill until firm and break into pieces.

CHOCOLATE-COVERED FRUIT

What You Need:

Fruit: choose from bananas, strawberries, pineapple, apples, etc.
1 12-oz. package of chocolate morsels (or chopped chocolate bar)
3 Tbsp. margarine.

Saucepan or double boiler
Toothpicks
Waxed paper
Potholder
Measuring spoon

What You Do:

1. Melt chocolate and margarine on top of stove in saucepan or double boiler. Use low heat and stir to prevent burning.

2. Put fruit on toothpicks and dip into chocolate. Place on waxed paper and chill in refrigerator until chocolate hardens.

CHOCOLATE NUT-RAISIN CLUSTERS

What You Need:

6 oz. package semi-sweet
   chocolate chips (or chopped
   chocolate bar)
1½ cups shelled walnuts
1 cup raisins

Spoon
Saucepan or double boiler
Waxed paper
Potholder
Measuring cup

What You Do:

1. Melt chocolate over warm water in double boiler, or in saucepan over low heat.

2. Stir in nuts and raisins.

3. Drop by teaspoonfuls onto waxed paper and chill.

   Makes 12-18

DRINKS

BANANA SHAKE

What You Need:

2 cups milk
1 banana, sliced
1 Tbsp. honey

Measuring cup and spoon
Blender
Glass

What You Do:

1. Place all ingredients into blender jar and whip on medium speed until well mixed.
2. Pour into tall glass and enjoy.

BERRY SHAKE

What You Need:

1 cup strawberries (frozen)
1 cup milk
1 Tbsp. honey

What You Do:

Follow directions above.

70

COOLERS

GRAPE SPRITZER

Fill a glass half full with grape juice. Add seltzer and stir.

LEMONADE

In a small pitcher, combine 2 cups seltzer, ½ cup lemon juice and 2 tablespoons honey. Add ice and mix.

CHOCOLATE EGG CREAM

Stir 2 tablespoons chocolate syrup into ½ cup milk. Add club soda to top of glass. Stir.

Spoon
Glass
Measuring cup and spoon

"My Favorite Recipes"